The Joy Journal

Created by
Jennifer Peterson, PhD, PCC

Published by Tail Feather Coaching / MoxieQuest
www.MoxieQuest.us

Author photo by Anne Lloyd

ISBN: 978-0-692-11401-8

Printed in the United States of America by Bookmobile

"Tu blave..."

Dedicated to you, Peter.
Thanks for helping me find my Joy!

The Joy Journal

Table of Contents

Introduction: Finding Joy

I found Joy.

She came to me in the form of a big black horse.

I had asked a friend to find me an exceptional driving horse and two days later I got the call. Thinking the search for a new horse would take at least a couple of months; I was not prepared to move so quickly. He told me all about the horse's pedigree and vast driving experience.

Finally I asked him, "What is her name?"

His response was, "Joy."

Of course her name is Joy because that is exactly what I was really looking for. My fascination and love of horses has been with me for as long as I can remember. I learned to ride when I was five years old and would muck stalls just to have the chance to be around them. When I was 14, I finally got my own pony. I had found joy.

In February of 1983, my life changed forever. I broke my neck in a downhill skiing accident and became a quadriplegic. I was left with limited use of my arms, shoulders and wrists, while the rest of my body is paralyzed from the chest down. It was a devastating time and I had lost my joy.

Thanks to the support of family and friends, I was able to put the pieces of my life back together. I've been in a wheelchair for over 30 years and it truly takes a small village to make my life full and possible. My biggest champion is Peter Berridge. He is my soul mate, better half, husband, and believer in dreams. So very much of my success can be attributed to him and his involvement. Throughout the years that we have been together, I've come up with some pretty crazy ideas and he helps turn them into reality. I found joy again!

Even with so much good, there is still a deep wound. Living life with a disability is hard. There are moments where it wears me out along with tiring out all of my great family and friends. Pete even needs a get away from the total physical dependency from time to time. It is a 24-7 venture that requires attentiveness, strength, and perseverance.

Unfortunately I cannot escape or take a break from being disabled. At my worst moments, it feels like I'm trapped in a broken body...a body for which I had so many dreams and wishes.

The high-powered able-bodied girl of my youth is gone and I desperately miss her. My grief in losing her can be overwhelming. In a split second, the sadness can stop me in my tracks and take my breath away leaving me a sobbing mess.

Some of my worst moments have been lying in bed either waiting to fall asleep at night or waiting for someone to get me up in the morning. Fully awake and not able to move. Perfectly still. Vulnerable. Waiting. Stuck. Trying hard to not let my thoughts run away with me. What if there's a fire? What if there's a tornado? Would someone save me? I know these thoughts are irrational and yet they get reinforced every day on the evening news. Fear can be more paralyzing than my actual disability. The vulnerability triggers a deep insecurity of being abandoned.

It is normal to want to run away and hide from the bad stuff and yet this is not a sustainable option. It took me a long time to figure out that emotions are my friend (all emotions- not just the happy ones). These physiological responses are my body's way of giving me valuable information. To engage with grief taught me that I love deeply. To wrestle with frustration taught me that I have

values and boundaries. To cry in sadness taught me that I have passion, hopes and dreams.

My grief and loss will never "go away" or "get better" and I will never "get over it." Parts of me are broken and scared and the scares are reminders of battles fought and wounds received. Loss is loss and the hard stuff cannot be fixed - it can only be held. So I hold the love and loss that I have for my previous life gently - with kindness and compassion - as if I was holding a baby kitten that just fell asleep in my arms. I allow the emotional energy to move through me releasing as much as I can in the moment.

The biggest lesson that I have learned through all of my life adventures is resilience. Life can be really hard sometimes and nothing can fix it or make it easier. If we love, our hearts will break. If we put ourselves out there, we will fail. If we choose to be big and bold, we will get pushed down. Sorrow, grief and loss are important elements to living a full life because if we play it safe (never love, never challenge ourselves or never take risks), we'll never get hurt. But here's the deal - we'll also be alone, unfulfilled and dull.

Resilience is our ability to bounce back from adversity. It is the inner voice that whispers to the universe - "I'll try again tomorrow." It is the indescribable energy that makes us strive for more even when things seem impossible.

For me, having horses in my life again was an impossible dream. They can spook and move fast and I am physically limited and move slow. I kept this dream hidden for many years. Hidden even from myself. Losing horses once was extremely painful and I wasn't sure I was willing to risk it again. The first person I told this secret dream to was Pete. He didn't laugh like I thought he might. His reaction was quite the opposite. He encouraged and supported me and said, "If that's what you want to do, let's make it happen." He is my champion and truly makes my life possible.

Fast-forward five years, I now have Joy.

When I'm driving Joy (from a wheelchair accessible cart), I'm living into my biggest and boldest self. Every time I'm in the cart, I am physically doing something that I thought was impossible. It never gets old and always brings a smile to my face and warms my heart. I am saying yes to my greatest desires. I am cultivating joy.

Working with Joy allows me to open up and get in touch with the deepest part of my wounded self. We are connected. I ask and she listens. She is beautiful and powerful and together we fly!

As an executive coach, my favorite coaching question is, "what makes your heart sing?" Or to quote Miracle Max from Princess Bride, "Whatcha got that's worth living for?" I challenge my clients to live fully just as I am trying to do in my own life. This is not an easy task. This is the hard work of life. Recognizing, owning and claiming what you love and then doing something with it is stepping right into courage and vulnerability.

With life, there are no guarantees. If we put ourselves out there and risk, we could look silly, be humiliated, lose out, get hurt, or worse of all - fail. And yet, in building resilience, we may still find small moments of joy that can be cultivated. We can slowly see growth through our pain. We can get back up and try again. The rainbows come only after the storm.

My relationship with Joy inspired the creation of this journal. She reminds me to seek out and notice joyful moments. Noticing the small things that make me smile can lay the foundation of creating more peace, calm, and life enjoyment.

Out of my relationship with Joy came this journal. She reminds me that we create our own Joy by noticing and becoming more aware. By speaking my truth, I found Joy.

So as I continue to challenge myself, I also challenge you. Use this Joy Journal to find your small moments of Joy. It is within your power if you choose to step into it!

Here's to cultivating more Joy!

Much love to you,

Jenny

Welcome!

Hello! I'm excited to have you join me on this journey of cultivating joy. This daily Joy Journal was inspired by interactions with my Morgan horse, Greentree Night Joy – we call her "Joy" for short. Joy came into my life in October 2016 and since then has assisted me in creating many joy-filled moments. Having "Joy" in my life created an ongoing metaphor of looking for and cultivating more "joy." With her as my partner, I have become more intentional about finding joy in the smallest of ways. This process has changed my life for the better and I want to share this with you.

The creation of this journal was also supported by research generated through Positive Psychology which is the scientific study of what is "right" with us. For many decades, much of the research on humans was focused on what was wrong with us so that we could cure or fix these problems. This has been a noble pursuit however it has only showed us half of the human life equation. Beginning in the mid 1990's, researchers began studying things like happiness, passion, fulfillment and love. When it comes to knowing what makes us happy, healthy and joyful, we are just scratching the surface on rich and meaningful data.

Marcus Buckingham, British author, speaker, and business consultant, describes this well:

> *"Everywhere we look we seem to think that excellence is the opposite of failure. We study divorce to learn about marriage. We study unhappy customers to learn about the happy ones. We study disgruntled employees to learn how to engage employees. We study depression, neurosis, psychosis to learn about joy...Everywhere you look we seem to think that good is the opposite of bad. If you want good, you should study bad and invert it. We're wrong...if you study bad and invert it you get not bad. Studying depression teaches you a lot about depression. It tells you nothing about joy."*
> *(Buckingham, 2007)*

Thankfully Positive Psychology is making scientific strides in generating tangible data to support what makes life worth living. Much of the research focuses on our strengths and asks about what is going well in our lives so that we can "thrive and flourish" (Haidt, 2000).

Your Joy Journal was designed to assist you in creating an intentional practice of cultivating joy. In doing so, you will engage with the following activities and behaviors that science says is good for you:

- Gratitude, joy & positive emotions
- Emotional intelligence
- Self-compassion and self-kindness
- Intentional focus and letting in the good
- The law of little things
- Social support and connecting with others
- Creating new habits

To read more about Positive Psychology and the supporting research that was used in creating your Joy Journal, please see the research and reference sections in the back of this book.

The Purpose of Your Joy Journal

The purpose of The Joy Journal is to give you a practical tool to put this research into action and use it to build "good" in your own life.

The Design of Your Joy Journal

Your Joy Journal is designed for you to create an ongoing writing and reflection practice so that you will become more intentional about cultivating joy. Each journal page has three sections:

- A daily quote along with two reflective questions
- A morning section of questions
- An evening section of questions

The daily quote allows you to be inspired by someone else's words and then answer two thoughtful questions to apply it in your own life. The morning and evening questions allow you to create a beginning and end of the day ritual of writing and reflecting. Each section was designed to take 3-5 minutes (on average) so that you'll spend approximately 15 minutes daily focusing on joy. You'll notice that some of the questions and thought prompts are the same from day to day and week to week -- and some are different. The goal is to have some repetition along with some novelty so you won't get bored. The journal layout is for a total of ten weeks or 70 days as the new research shows that it takes a minimum of 66 days to create a new habit (Lally, et. al., 2010). To learn more about this, see the research section in the back.

Only One Rule – Make it Your Own!

This Joy Journal was created for YOU! From the white front and back covers, to the deliberate white space and doodle pages, to the daily quote and questions – its all up to you in how you use this and make this journal your own. Right now, I give you permission to make this Joy Journal your own! Here are some

suggestions:

- You can choose a deep dive into Joy and complete all three sections everyday or you can choose to do only one or two sections every once and a while.
- You can mix it up and choose different aspects each day.
- You can do all three sections in one sitting or you can spread it out to three times a day.

It's all up to you and there is no right or wrong way to cultivate joy – only your way!

The cover is white so that you can decorate it however you'd like. You can leave it the way it is or use paint, markers, and/or decoupage to make it bright and colorful – you decide. You can glue an envelope to the inside front or back cover and create a Joy Pocket to have a specific place for you to "collect" joy. Please put anything that fits in the envelope that brings you joy or makes you smile. Suggestions include: photograph(s), a dried flower and/or leaf, ticket stubs, money, a note from someone, a quote, and/or a note to yourself.

Throughout your Joy Journal, there are random blank pages for doodling, coloring, and/or pasting pictures or whatever you'd like. You can fill these with notes, thoughts, or just leave them blank. There are also images sprinkled throughout for you to color (or not). Lastly, there are random reflection pages for you to capture any changes in your thinking, feeling and behaviors as a result of your engagement with your Joy Journaling practice. Again, go ahead and answer all of the questions - or not!

How to Use Your Joy Journal – Be creative!

You get to decide how you want to use your Joy Journal. There are many ways to go about this and here are a few suggestions:

- Start at the beginning of the journal and go page by page, completing one journal page each day
- Start at the end of the journal and go page by page backwards, completing one journal page each day
- Flip open the book randomly and complete that page for the day (if you flip it open and you've already completed that page, flip it open again or just turn the page)
- Complete just the inspirational quote section each day
- Complete all three sections in the morning
- Complete all three sections in the evening
- Write in your Joy Journal daily, weekly or monthly – or randomly whenever you have time!

Joy Journal Frequently Asked Questions

- *Do I have to write in my journal everyday?*

Research shows that when people create a routine and do something often, they get better at it. So it is up to you. If daily writing is too much to start with, try completing it twice a week. When you are successful with that, try adding additional days. The idea is to enjoy what you ARE doing versus focusing on what you are not doing. If you enjoy this, most likely you will do it more often. If you make your Joy Journal a chore, most likely you will not want to complete it.

- *What if mornings (or evenings) are best for me?*

Then write in your Joy Journal then – complete all of the sections or only finish one, or two sections…it is ALL up to you! The most important aspect is to make this process your own. There is no right or wrong way to cultivate joy. Figure out what works best for you and do more of that!

- *Suggestion: If you are a morning person...*

Begin your Joy Journal by completing the evening section from the day before. Start with a reflection from the previous day – fill-in those answers – and then move onto the new day's morning questions and inspirational quote. By reflecting on what worked and what didn't work from the day before, this might help you in setting your intention for the new day and what you may try again and/or try to do differently. Then you could wrap up your reflective writing session by looking ahead to the evening questions to see what is coming next.

- *Suggestion: If you are an evening person...*

Go ahead and fill-in the full Joy Journal page for the whole day. Stop and reflect on how your day progressed and answer both the morning and evening sections – just change the morning questions into past tense. For example, if the question is: What am I grateful for? You can change that to: What was I grateful for? Then you could wrap up your reflective writing by answering the quote questions (or you can start with the quote questions!).

- *Can I read or look ahead in my Joy Journal?*

Of course you can! You can read ahead, skip pages, jump right to a coloring page...again, it is all up to you!

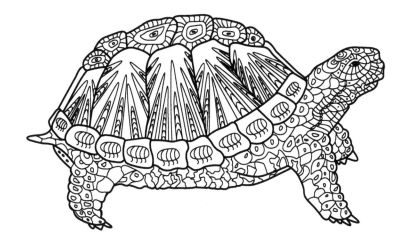

- *What happens if I forget to write in my journal for a day (or two, or three…)?*

Great news! Just start again. This Joy Journal is not about being perfect. It is about YOU being YOU. We all forget or run out of time. The great thing is that your Joy Journal will be waiting for you whenever you need or want it. If you miss an evening, you can "catch-up" the next day or you can start there the next morning or leave it blank and move on – the main goal is to make it work for you and have fun with it.

- *What if I don't like one of the questions?*

Change it! Make up your own question. Cross it out and write in something else. Or don't answer it at all and leave it blank!

- *What if the question does not apply to me?*

Change it! Make up your own question. Cross it out and write in something else. Or don't answer it at all and leave it blank!

- *What if I don't have an answer to one of the questions?*

Write about what you do feel. It does not have to be perfect or all tied up with a pretty bow. If you had a crappy day, be honest and write about that…and then, once that is out of your system, challenge yourself to find one small thing that brought you joy. Was there one little thing that made you smile? Somedays we may have to look harder than others and then write that down too.

- *What if my honest answer to a question is "I don't know"?*

It is perfectly okay to begin at this place of not knowing. Your job then is to go out and find out. Leaving your answer as "I don't know" is selling yourself short. Have faith in yourself that you can find some sort of answer even if you feel that it is a little bit non traditional or different than others!

- *What if I have a hard time setting an intention?*

For some, this comes easily and for others it does not. Some days may feel more purposeful while others may not. To set your intention for the day, reflect upon how it is you would like to show up. Some examples could be: patient, peaceful, loving, with good boundaries, with self-compassion, open, lighthearted, honest, authentic. You can take it from here.

- *What if I don't feel Joyful?*

That's ok and normal. Emotions are like thoughts in the fact that they come and go, you can't control them, and everyone experiences them (even if they say they don't). A way to think about emotions is that they are data that your body is using to communicate with you. So instead of being frustrated with your anger or anxiety, you could "mine the data" and ask yourself about what the emotion is trying to tell you. For example, resentment usually means that a boundary of some sort was crossed - you said yes when you really wanted to say no. Now that you have figured this out, resentment can become your friend as it is trying to inform and direct you on the choices you make.

The practice of cultivating joy can be a challenge especially if you are experiencing stress, loss, or grief and yet, this may be exactly when you need it most. It is a myth to think that you can be happy all of the time. As an emotional being that sometimes thinks, you would be losing much of life's richness if you only felt happy, joy or loving emotions. There is passion in anger and the wisdom of this emotion can fuel you to make change. Fear is your most primitive emotion and helps you to understand threat or danger. You don't want to turn these off even though they can be very uncomfortable to feel. What you do want to do is to engage with the wisdom of these emotions, learn from them, and use this valuable information to inform your actions and behaviors. Cultivating joy is an act of stepping into emotional intelligence. It is a momentary practice of letting in the good no matter what is happening in your life. It might take awhile to notice a small smile or a glint of a giggle and yet, when it does show up, it will be worth the focus and hard work.

- *Why does the Joy Journal have so much white space?*
There are no lines in this Joy Journal because I want you to write where ever you want…at the top of the page, at the bottom, in the margins – write ALL over this Joy Journal. Make it your own. Write with one special pen. Write with multiple colors. Use a crayon! Do what ever makes you happy AND write all over this thing. You have permission to color outside the lines!

Granting Permission

Speaking of permission, what permission(s) do you need to give yourself to cultivate joy?

Here are a few examples:
- To play and have fun
- To be imperfect and write in my journal when I have time
- To be kind and forgiving if I miss a day
- To not know my answers to some of the questions and writing down something anyway
- If I drop off from using my Joy Journal, allow myself to just begin again where I left off with no judgment

Working with your Joy Journal is not a race or a competition. It is not about being perfect or mechanically going through the motions of writing down meaningless stuff everyday. It is about self-reflection, honestly, courage and vulnerability. It's about being imperfect and messy and allowing yourself to drop any social masks that dictate how you think you're supposed to be. The Joy Journal is solely for you to use however you wish. It offers one guarantee – it will always be there for you when you want it!

Time to jump in and get started!

"Courage starts with showing up
and letting ourselves be seen."
-- *Brené Brown*

How can I let others see more of the real me?

What holds me back from going all in?

Morning:

Where will I look for joy today?

My self kindness message to myself for today is:

Evening:

Where did I find joy today?

What is one thing that I enjoyed today?

"'The desire to create is one of the
deepest yearnings of the human soul."
-- Elder Uchtdorf

What in me seeks expression?

How might I let it be expressed?

Morning:

Who will I say thank you to today?

What would make today a good day?

Evening:

What was one simple joy that I experienced today?

Who did I appreciate today?

"I've learned that people will forget what you said,
people will forget what you did, but people will
never forget how you made them feel."
-- *Maya Angelou*

Who have I hugged lately?

Who have I helped feel good about themselves?

Morning:

Today I am grateful for:

I will add joy to the world today by:

Evening:

What is one thing that made me smile today?

What is one new thing I learned today?

"An open heart is
an open mind."
-- *Dalai Lama*

How open is my heart?

How open is my mind?

Morning:

One of my strengths is:

One of my values that I live by is:

Evening:

Who did I trust today?

Who trusted me?

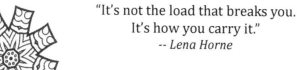

"It's not the load that breaks you.
It's how you carry it."
-- Lena Horne

How heavy is my load?

What can I set down to lighten the load?

Morning:

What do I look foward to today?

How can I build in quite time today?

Evening:

How did I contribute to the success of others today?

How was I generous today?

"Sometimes the most urgent thing you can
possibly do is take a complete rest."
-- Ashleigh Brilliant

How have I deeply rested lately?

How can I build in more moments of rest?

Morning:

How will I reach out for support today?

How will I help someone else today?

Evening:

What challenged me today to help me grow?

What is the kindest word that I can think of to describe me?

The Joy Journal

"Wherever you go,
there you are."
-- Zen saying

What are all of the things that are working in my life?

What makes my heart sing?

Morning:

What is one thing that's new that I will try today?

Who will I offer a hug to today?

Evening:

What's one thing that was successful today?

What did I enjoy most from today?

Doodle / Blank Page

"The conductor of an orchestra doesn't make a sound.
He depends for his power on his ability
to make other people powerful."
-- *Benjamin Zander*

How have I empowered others?

Who has empowered me?

Morning:

How will I spread a small amount of joy today?

Who will I send love to today?

Evening:

What was something that pleasently surprized me today?

What went well today?

"You can't achieve your life's purpose
by trying to achieve your life's purpose."
-- Victor Frankel

How might I relax more and be open to new possibilities?

Where might I be trying too hard?

Morning:

Who will I reach out to today?

How will I be kind to myself today?

Evening:

How did I stretch myself to go beyond my comfort zone today?

What did I love today?

"To live a creative life,
we must lose our fear of being wrong. "
-- Joseph Chilton Pearce

How can I let go of needing to be right?

When I fail, how can I value that as much as success?

Morning:

What choice do I look forward to today?

What is one thing that I want from today?

Evening:

What is one thing from today that I can savor for 60 seconds?

What inspired me today?

The Joy Journal

"Anxiety is the
hand maiden of creativity."
-- T.S. Eliot

What is the message of my anxiety?

How might I harness this energy for creativity?

Morning:

How would I like to grow today?

What makes me smile right now?

Evening:

What made me laugh out loud today?

How was I resilient today?

"Initiative is doing the right thing
without being told."
-- Victor Hugo

What is one thing I know I need to do?

How can I move forward?

Morning:

How can I be courageous today?

How can I be vulnerable today?

Evening:

Who did I smile at today?

How did I share joy today?

"Peace cannot be achieved through violence,
it can only be attained through understanding."
-- *Ralph Waldo Emerson*

How can I better understand another's point of view?

How can I expand my thoughts to include other's
perspectives that are different than mine?

Morning:

How will I slow down today?

What stength will I share today?

Evening:

What was I able to let go of today?

What was beautiful about today?

"The more that you read, the more things you will know.
The more that you learn,
the more places you'll go."
-- Dr. Seuss

What more do I want to learn about?

Where might I need to go to learn about it?

Morning:

What is one small thing I will do for myself today?

What is somethng that I am grateful for?

Evening:

Who or what did I enjoy most today?

How did I notice the smallest of joys today?

Reflections Page

Where have I found joy?

What have I learned about myself?

How am I shifting? Changing?

What do I want to do more of?

How can I apply this?

What makes my heart sing?

What makes me smile?

Doodle / Blank Page

"Let go of your mind and then be mindful.
Close your ears and listen!"
-- Jalaluddin Rumi

How can I experience this moment through my body?

What wisdom is my physical body sharing with me?

Morning:

Where will I look for joy today?

My self kindness message to myself for today is:

Evening:

Where did I find joy today?

What is one thing that I enjoyed today?

"Letting there be room for not knowing
is the most important thing of all."
-- *Pema Chödrön*

How can I let go of needing to know?

How can I relax into not knowing?

Morning:

Who will I say thank you to today?

What would make today a good day?

Evening:

What was one simple joy that I experienced today?

Who did I say thank you to today?

"Everything that slows us down and forces patience,
everything that sets us back into
the slow circles of nature, is a help."
-- May Sarton

How have I slowed down lately?

How did it feel when I did this?

Morning:

Today I am grateful for:

I will add joy to the world today by:

Evening:

What is one thing that made me smile today?

What is one new thing I learned today?

"If the doors of perception were cleansed,
everything would appear to man as it is, infinite."
-- William Blake

How might I be living small?

How can I make my world bigger?

Morning:

One of my strengths is:

One of my values that I live by is:

Evening:

Who did I trust today?

Who trusted me?

"When one tugs at a single thing in nature,
he finds it attached to the rest of the world."
-- John Muir

How am I interconnected with others, animals and nature?

What is one thing I could do to deepen my connection?

Morning:

What do I look foward to today?

How can I build in quite time today?

Evening:

How did I contribute to the success of others today?

How was I generous today?

"Gratefulness is that fullness of life
for which we are all thirsting."
-- *Brother David Steindl-Rast*

What am I most grateful for?

How can I savor this for 60 seconds?

Morning:

How will I reach out for support today?

How will I help someone else today?

Evening:

What challenged me today to help me grow?

What is the kindest word that I can think of to describe me?

"The wound is the place
where the Light enters you."
-- Rumi

What is one of my wounds?

How does letting the light in impact my wound?

Morning:

What is one thing that's new that I will try today?

Who will I offer a hug to today?

Evening:

What's one thing that was successful today?

What did I enjoy most from today?

Reflections Page

Where have I found joy?

What have I learned about myself?

How am I shifting? Changing?

What do I want to do more of?

How can I apply this?

What makes my heart sing?

What makes me smile?

Doodle / Blank Page

The Joy Journal   *Date:*

"Wisdom
begins in wonder."
-- Socrates

What am I in awe of?

What do I wonder most about?

Morning:

How will I spread a small amount of joy today?

Who will I send love to today?

Evening:

What was something that pleasently surprized me today?

What went well today?

"You can have no greater or lesser dominion
than the one over yourself. The greatest deception men
suffer is from their own opinions."
-- Leonardo da Vinci

How might my critic get in my way?

How might my opinions be more open and less judgmental?

Morning:

Who will I reach out to today?

How will I be kind to myself today?

Evening:

How did I stretch myself to go beyond my comfort zone today?

What did I love today?

"If you want something you never had,
you must be willing to do
something you've never done."
-- Lisa Fenn

What is one new thing that I've always wanted to try?

How might I stretch myself in a new direction?

Morning:

What choice do I look forward to today?

What is one thing that I want from today?

Evening:

What is one thing from today that I can savor for 60 seconds?

What inspired me today?

The Joy Journal

"The secret of getting ahead
is getting started."
-- Mark Twain

What is something small or big I want to achieve?

What is one small thing I could do today to get started?

Morning:

How would I like to grow today?

What makes me smile right now?

Evening:

What made me laugh out loud today?

How was I resilient today?

"The dark does not destroy the light;
it defines it. It's our fear of the dark
that casts our joy into the shadows."
-- *Brené Brown*

How am I afraid of the dark?

What scares me the most?

Morning:

How can I be courageous today?

How can I be vulnerable today?

Evening:

Who did I smile at today?

How did I share joy today?

The Joy Journal

"Joy in looking and comprehending
is nature's most beautiful gift."
-- Albert Einstein

What gift from nature have I experienced lately?

How can I look for more of these gifts?

Morning:

How will I slow down today?

What stength will I share today?

Evening:

What was I able to let go of today?

What was beautiful about today?

"I continue to keep the cornucopia
of technology at arm's length, so that
I can more easily remember who I am."
-- *Kevin Kelly*

When was the last time I completely unplugged from technology?

How might I build in more moments of technology disconnect?

Morning:

What is one small thing I will do for myself today?

What is somethng that I am grateful for?

Evening:

Who or what did I enjoy most today?

How did I notice the smallest of joys today?

Reflections Page

Where have I found joy?

What have I learned about myself?

How am I shifting? Changing?

What do I want to do more of?

How can I apply this?

What makes my heart sing?

What makes me smile?

Doodle / Blank Page

"When educating the minds of our youth,
we must not forget to educate their hearts."
-- Dalai Lama

How might I inspire another person's heart?

How can I create an environment of openness?

Morning:

Where will I look for joy today?

My self kindness message to myself for today is:

Evening:

Where did I find joy today?

What is one thing that I enjoyed today?

"This above all: to thine own self be true,
and it must follow, as the night the day,
thou canst not then be false to any man."
-- *William Shakespeare*

How can I be most honest with myself?

What does my authenticity look and feel like?

Morning:

Who will I say thank you to today?

What would make today a good day?

Evening:

What was one simple joy that I experienced today?

Who did I say thank you to today?

"Just because a man lacks the use of his eyes
doesn't mean he lacks vision."
-- Stevie Wonder

What is my vision?

How might I deepen what I see?

Morning:

Today I am grateful for:

I will add joy to the world today by:

Evening:

What is one thing that made me smile today?

What is one new thing I learned today?

The Joy Journal

"Only love can be divided endlessly
and still not diminish."
-- *Anne Morrow Lindbergh*

How does love multiply in my world?

How do I share love with others?

Morning:

One of my strengths is:

One of my values that I live by is:

Evening:

Who did I trust today?

Who trusted me?

"Do every act of your life
as though it is the last act of your life."
-- Marcus Aurelius

What is most important to me in my life?

How do I make this a priority?

Morning:

What do I look foward to today?

How can I build in quite time today?

Evening:

How did I contribute to the success of others today?

How was I generous today?

"Acceptance of one's life has nothing to do with resignation; it does not mean running away from the struggle. On the contrary it means accepting it as it comes...To accept is to say yes to life in its entirety."
-- *Paul Tournier*

What might I be struggling with?

How might I ask another for help?

Morning:

How will I reach out for support today?

How will I help someone else today?

Evening:

What challenged me today to help me grow?

What is the kindest word that I can think of to describe me?

"The bee is more honored than other animals,
not because she labors,
but because she labors for others."
-- *Saint John Chrysostom*

What have I done in service for another?

What labor could I do for someone else's benefit?

Morning:

What is one thing that's new that I will try today?

Who will I offer a hug to today?

Evening:

What's one thing that was successful today?

What did I enjoy most from today?

Reflections Page

Where have I found joy?

What have I learned about myself?

How am I shifting? Changing?

What do I want to do more of?

How can I apply this?

What makes my heart sing?

What makes me smile?

Doodle / Blank Page

"Creativity is the way I share
my soul with the world."
-- *Brené Brown*

How am I creative?

How can I share more of this with others?

Morning:

How will I spread a small amount of joy today?

Who will I send love to today?

Evening:

What was something that pleasently surprized me today?

What went well today?

"True peace between nations will only happen
when there is true peace within people's souls."
-- *Native American Proverb*

How can I focus more on peace?

How might I help spread peace?

Morning:

Who will I reach out to today?

How will I be kind to myself today?

Evening:

How did I stretch myself to go beyond my comfort zone today?

What did I love today?

"Love is the
guardian deity of everything."
-- *Morihei Ueshiba*

How does love show up in my life?

What do I love?

Morning:

What choice do I look forward to today?

What is one thing that I want from today?

Evening:

What is one thing from today that I can savor for 60 seconds?

What inspired me today?

"Wilderness is not a luxury
but a necessity of the human spirit."
-- *Edward Abbey*

How am I feeding my spirit?

What is the wildest thing I'd like to do?

Morning:

How would I like to grow today?

What makes me smile right now?

Evening:

What made me laugh out loud today?

How was I resilient today?

"We are each made for goodness, love and compassion.
Our lives are transformed as much as the world is
when we live with these truths."
-- Desmond Tutu

How have I shared my goodness, love and compassion?

How has this transformed others?

Morning:

How can I be courageous today?

How can I be vulnerable today?

Evening:

Who did I smile at today?

How did I share joy today?

"If it's painful, you become willing not just to
endure it but also to let it awaken your heart and
soften you. You learn to embrace it."
-- *Pema Chödrön*

What painfulness might I need to embrace?

What awareness is this painfulness offering me?

Morning:

How will I slow down today?

What stength will I share today?

Evening:

What was I able to let go of today?

What was beautiful about today?

"How we spend our hours
is how we spend our lives."
-- Laura Vanderkam

What do my hours look like?

How might I be more intentional with my time?

Morning:

What is one small thing I will do for myself today?

What is somethng that I am grateful for?

Evening:

Who or what did I enjoy most today?

How did I notice the smallest of joys today?

Reflections Page

Where have I found joy?

What have I learned about myself?

How am I shifting? Changing?

What do I want to do more of?

How can I apply this?

What makes my heart sing?

What makes me smile?

Doodle / Blank Page

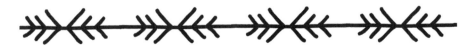

"Do all the good you can. By all the means you can. In all the
ways you can. In all the places you can. At all the times you can.
To all the people you can. As long as ever you can."
-- John Wesley

How can I be persistent in pursuit of my dreams?

What more can I give of myself?

Morning:

Where will I look for joy today?

My self kindness message to myself for today is:

Evening:

Where did I find joy today?

What is one thing that I enjoyed today?

The Joy Journal

"To travel is to
take a journey into
yourself."
-- Danny Kaye

What adventure is calling me?

What might I learn about myself on this journey?

Morning:

Who will I say thank you to today?

What would make today a good day?

Evening:

What was one simple joy that I experienced today?

Who did I say thank you to today?

"Believe what your heart tells you
when you ask, 'does this spark joy?'"
-- Marie Kondo

What makes my heart sing?

What makes my mouth smile?

Morning:

Today I am grateful for:

I will add joy to the world today by:

Evening:

What is one thing that made me smile today?

What is one new thing I learned today?

"Artists strive to free this true and spontaneous
self in their work. Creativity, meditation are
ways of freeing an inner voice."
-- Gloria Steinem

How have I listened to my inner voice?

What is it saying?

Morning:

One of my strengths is:

One of my values that I live by is:

Evening:

Who did I trust today?

Who trusted me?

"Being human is not about being any one particular way; it is about being as life creates you—with your own particular strengths and weaknesses, gifts and challenges, quirks and oddities."
-- *Kristen Neff*

What is my most outrageous quirk?

What is most odd about me?

Morning:

What do I look foward to today?

How can I build in quite time today?

Evening:

How did I contribute to the success of others today?

How was I generous today?

"Vulnerability is the birthplace
of innovation,
creativity and change."
-- Brené Brown

How have I been vulnerable?

What courage do I need to be vulnerable?

Morning:

How will I reach out for support today?

How will I help someone else today?

Evening:

What challenged me today to help me grow?

What is the kindest word that I can think of to describe me?

"Don't worry too much about what
other people think about you,
because they seldom do."
-- Fred Austin

How much does "what others think" stop me from doing something?

What if other's opinions did not matter, what would I do?

Morning:

What is one thing that's new that I will try today?

Who will I offer a hug to today?

Evening:

What's one thing that was successful today?

What did I enjoy most from today?

Reflections Page

Where have I found joy?

What have I learned about myself?

How am I shifting? Changing?

What do I want to do more of?

How can I apply this?

What makes my heart sing?

What makes me smile?

Doodle / Blank Page

"Happiness lies in the joy of
achievement and the
thrill of creative effort."
-- Franklin D. Roosevelt

What have I accomplished that has made me feel good?

How can I linger with this feeling to make it last longer?

Morning:

How will I spread a small amount of joy today?

Who will I send love to today?

Evening:

What was something that pleasently surprized me today?

What went well today?

The Joy Journal

"Let us always meet each other
with smile, for the smile is
the beginning of love."
-- *Mother Teresa*

How can I share my smile more?

What gets in the way of me expressing my genuine smile?

Morning:

Who will I reach out to today?

How will I be kind to myself today?

Evening:

How did I stretch myself to go beyond my comfort zone today?

What did I love today?

"Whatever you can do or dream you can,
begin it. Boldness has genius,
magic, and power in it."
-- *Johann Wolfgang von Goethe*

What dream can I begin?

What do I need to take that first step?

Morning:

What choice do I look forward to today?

What is one thing that I want from today?

Evening:

What is one thing from today that I can savor for 60 seconds?

What inspired me today?

"You have not lived today until you
have done something for someone
who can never repay you."
-- *John Bunyan*

What is something I could do that is anonymous?

How might this anonymous gift make me feel?

Morning:

How would I like to grow today?

What makes me smile right now?

Evening:

What made me laugh out loud today?

How was I resilient today?

"If you want to touch the past, touch a rock.
If you want to touch the present, touch a flower.
If you want to touch the future, touch a life."
-- Author Unknown

How have I made a difference to someone else?

Who has made a difference for me?

Morning:

How can I be courageous today?

How can I be vulnerable today?

Evening:

Who did I smile at today?

How did I share joy today?

"You can find magic wherever
you look. Sit back and relax,
all you need is a book."
-- *Dr. Seuss*

What book, story or movie is magical for me?

What is the message of the magic?

Morning:

How will I slow down today?

What stength will I share today?

Evening:

What was I able to let go of today?

What was beautiful about today?

"Who looks outside, dreams;
who looks inside, awakes."
-- Carl Jung

What are my inner strengths?

How have I used these to deepen my awareness?

Morning:

what is one small thing I will do for myself today?

What is somethng that I am grateful for?

Evening:

Who or what did I enjoy most today?

How did I notice the smallest of joys today?

Reflections Page

Where have I found joy?

What have I learned about myself?

How am I shifting? Changing?

What do I want to do more of?

How can I apply this?

What makes my heart sing?

What makes me smile?

Doodle / Blank Page

"What you give, you will receive,
although it might sometimes come
from the place you least expect."
-- *Paulo Coelho*

What gifts have I shared?

What gifts have I received?

Morning:

Where will I look for joy today?

My self kindness message to myself for today is:

Evening:

Where did I find joy today?

What is one thing that I enjoyed today?

"The soul should always stand ajar,
ready to welcome
the ecstatic experience."
-- *Emily Dickinson*

What has surprised me lately?

How might I open up more?

Morning:

Who will I say thank you to today?

What would make today a good day?

Evening:

What was one simple joy that I experienced today?

Who did I say thank you to today?

"I am only one, but I am one. I cannot do everything,
but I can do something. And I will not let what
I cannot do interfere with what I can do."
-- Edward Everett Hale

What do I want to do today?

How will I make that happen?

Morning:

Today I am grateful for:

I will add joy to the world today by:

Evening:

What is one thing that made me smile today?

What is one new thing I learned today?

"The future belongs to those
who believe in the beauty
of their dreams."
-- *Eleanor Roosevelt*

What are my beautiful dreams?

How can I live into those dreams?

Morning:

One of my strengths is:

One of my values that I live by is:

Evening:

Who did I trust today?

Who trusted me?

"Not everything that can be
counted counts, and not everything
that counts can be counted."
-- *William Bruce Cameron*

What matters most to me?

How do I count my blessings?

Morning:

What do I look foward to today?

How can I build in quite time today?

Evening:

How did I contribute to the success of others today?

How was I generous today?

The Joy Journal

"Whatever inspiration is,
it's born from a continuous
'I don't know.'"
-- Wislawa Szymborska

How can I be more curious?

How can I lean into "not knowing?"

Morning:

How will I reach out for support today?

How will I help someone else today?

Evening:

What challenged me today to help me grow?

What is the kindest word that I can think of to describe me?

"Clear your
mind of can't."
-- Samuel Johnson

What would I do if I knew I couldn't fail?

What would I need to do even if I knew I would fail?

Morning:

What is one thing that's new that I will try today?

Who will I offer a hug to today?

Evening:

What's one thing that was successful today?

What did I enjoy most from today?

Reflections Page

Where have I found joy?

What have I learned about myself?

How am I shifting? Changing?

What do I want to do more of?

How can I apply this?

What makes my heart sing?

What makes me smile?

Doodle / Blank Page

"If you judge people,
you have no time
to love them."
-- *Mother Teresa*

How have I been judgmental of others lately?

What is one thing I have in common with someone I have judged?

Morning:

How will I spread a small amount of joy today?

Who will I send love to today?

Evening:

What was something that pleasently surprized me today?

What went well today?

"The most important thing
is remembering
the most important thing."
-- Suzuki Roshi

What is my "most important thing?"

How can I cultivate more of that "most important thing?"

Morning:

Who will I reach out to today?

How will I be kind to myself today?

Evening:

How did I stretch myself to go beyond my comfort zone today?

What did I love today?

"When you like yourself, you tend to be
cheerful; when you dislike yourself,
you tend to be depressed."
-- *Kristen Neff*

What three things do I like best about myself?

How have I been kind to myself lately?

Morning:

What choice do I look forward to today?

What is one thing that I want from today?

Evening:

What is one thing from today that I can savor for 60 seconds?

What inspired me today?

The Joy Journal

"Act as if what you do
makes a difference.
It does."
-- *William James*

How do I want to contribute?

What is one small step that I can do toward that?

Morning:

How would I like to grow today?

What makes me smile right now?

Evening:

What made me laugh out loud today?

How was I resilient today?

"We must shift our allegiances from fear to curiosity, from attachment to letting go, from control to trust, and from entitlement to humility."
-- *Angeles Arrien*

How can I be more curious and let go?

How can I trust more and be humble?

Morning:

How can I be courageous today?

How can I be vulnerable today?

Evening:

Who did I smile at today?

How did I share joy today?

"I say yes when I mean no
and the
wrinkle grows."
-- *Naomi Shihab Nye*

What might I need to let go of to make room for something else?

What have I said yes to when I really meant to say no?

Morning:

How will I slow down today?

What stength will I share today?

Evening:

What was I able to let go of today?

What was beautiful about today?

"He who has a why
to live for can bear
with almost any how."
-- Victor Frankl

What is my "why" to live for?

How do I cherish this?

Morning:

What is one small thing I will do for myself today?

What is somethng that I am grateful for?

Evening:

Who or what did I enjoy most today?

How did I notice the smallest of joys today?

Doodle / Blank Page

Research

Positive Psychology Research topics:
- Gratitude, Joy and Positive Emotions
- Emotional intelligence
- Self-compassion and Self-kindness
- Intentional focus and Letting in the Good
- Social Support and Connecting with Others
- Creating new habits - 66 days!

Positive Psychology: Introduction

The creation and design of The Joy Journal was influenced by research generated through Positive Psychology. This category of work is defined as:

"The scientific study of the strengths that enables individuals and communities to thrive. The field is founded on the belief that people want to lead meaningful and fulfilling lives, to cultivate what is best within themselves, and to enhance their experiences of love, work, and play" (PPC, 2017).

What began in 1998 as a call to action by Dr. Martin Seligman, then President of the American Psychological Association, has grown into thousands of experiments and research on topics such as flow, gratitude, grit, happiness, and resilience just to name a few. Below are a handful of topics along with short descriptions from this ever growing body of research that was foundational in developing The Joy Journal. Therefore, the purpose of The Joy Journal is to give you a practical tool to put this research into action and use it to build "good" in your own life. To learn more about Positive Psychology go to The Positive Psychology Center at The University of Pennsylvania: https://ppc.sas.upenn.edu

Gratitude

According to Emmons (2010), Professor of Psychology at UC Davis, gratitude has two parts – the first part is an affirmation of some level of goodness in our lives, and the second includes some sort of recognition that gratitude is generated from sources that are outside of ourselves. Thus by accepting the notion of gratitude, we acknowledge the good things in our lives and really notice that there is good stuff going on in our surrounding environments. When we create a practice of gratitude, we are being intentional in choosing to be aware of the stuff to be thankful for – no matter what is happening in our world. We could have a hard day at work and can still be thankful for the beautiful sunset or that our dog still loves us or that we are breathing..

Dr. Fredrickson (2009) suggests that: "Gratitude opens [our] hearts and carries the urge to give back – to do something good in return, either for the person who helped you or for someone else" (p. 41). Therefore, by first noticing that we are grateful and then creating a practice to reinforce this feeling of gratefulness, we may feel more contentment and a stronger desire to give back.

Professor Emmons' (2010) research demonstrates that when we regularly practice gratitude (like writing in a journal or counting our blessings), we may experience a whole host of positive health benefits such as:

Physical:
- Stronger immune system
- Less bothered by aches and pains
- Lower blood pressure
- Exercise more and take better care of your health
- Sleep longer and feel more refreshed

Psychological:
- Higher levels of positive emotions
- More alert, alive, and awake
- More joy and pleasure
- More optimism and happiness

Social:
- More helpful, generous, and compassionate
- More forgiving
- More outgoing
- Feel less lonely and isolated

Additional Supporting Research:
- The act of writing down our thoughts of gratitude can enhance flourishing because it helps us in creating meaning and/or deepen our understanding of our life experiences (Burton & King, 2009).
- Research indicates that scoring high on materialism correlates with decreased life-satisfaction and that creating a practice of gratitude is a potential intervention as it can lead to individuals feeling like they have all that they need (Tsang, et. al., 2014).

Joy

Many may think that gratitude, happiness and joy are the same feeling however, research shows that there are differences. Fearnley (2014) writes:

"Joy and happiness are wonderful feelings to experience, but are very different. Joy is more consistent and is cultivated internally. It comes when you make peace with who you are, why you are and how you are, whereas happiness tends to be externally triggered and is based on other people, things, places, thoughts and events."

While gratitude is the practice of being thankful, joy is momentary, fleeting, and quick. It can be a spark that happens spontaneously. It is the brief instant that you smiled. It can be the butterfly that fluttered by flashing its beautifully colored wings. Did you see it? Did you notice it? Did you feel it? And while there is a difference between gratitude, happiness and joy, there is still a relationship between them..

In a letter written by author CS Lewis in 1945, he describes real joy as something that "...jumps under ones ribs and tickles down one's back and makes one forget meals and keeps one (delightedly) sleepless o' nights."

J.D. Salinger, the author of Catcher in the Rye, wrote, "The fact is always obvious much too late, but the most singular difference between happiness and joy is that happiness is a solid and joy a liquid."

The goal of the Joy Journal is to create a practice of intentionally looking for the "fleeting sparks" in your world and to notice these moments. The search for joy can sometimes be elusive until we break it down into the smallest of components. Our job is to notice anything throughout our day that makes us smile, giggle, and/or pause. It could be a sunrise or sunset, a cat video, a child in the grocery store, a bird singing, or a white puffy cloud floating by. When we begin to see the small joys in our lives, we might be more effective in recognizing the larger joys. We each get to decide what brings us joy and once we build a habit of noticing joy, we are also enhancing our feelings of gratitude.

Additional Supporting Research:
- The research conducted by Lambert and colleagues at Brigham Young University show that discussing positive experiences can lead to heightened well being, increased overall life satisfaction and more energy (2012).

- Joy is a foundational emotion used by animals – and humans – that shows up when they are interacting and having fun (Bekoff, 2007).

Positive Emotions

Dr. Barbara Fredrickson from the University of North Carolina at Chapel Hill is one of the leading Positive Psychology researchers studying the effects of positive emotions and love. Her studies have shown that positive emotions lead to improved visual processing, creativity, resilience, performance, trust, memory for details, and better negotiation and decision-making (2001). These emotions transform us for the better and bring out the best in us. When we increase the amount of positive emotions that we experience, we change who we are and this takes effort, intention, and continual reinforcement, along with potential lifestyle changes (just like you would if you were wanting to eat healthier). In the words of Dr. Fredrickson, "If we increase our daily diet of positive emotions, we come out three months later being better, stronger, more resilient, more socially connected versions of ourselves" (2011).

Additional Supporting Research:
- Positive emotions have been linked with increased job performance, engagement, and satisfaction (Harter & Schmidt, 2003; Losada & Heaphy, 2004).
- Positive emotions, such as hope, optimism, gratitude, and joy have been found to open our hearts, broaden our minds and therefore, help us build new skills and additional resources for the future (Fredrickson, 1998).
- The degree to which people experience positive emotions in their lives, predicts whether people will languish or flourish (Fredrickson, 2011).

Emotional Intelligence

Emotional intelligence is "the ability to monitor one's own and others emotions, to discriminate among them, and to use the information to guide one's thinking and actions" (Salovey & Mayer, 1990, p. 185). Many of us may have a habit of stuffing down our emotions because we don't like to feel them, as they can be uncomfortable. The problem with this is that we are emotional beings that sometimes think (Brown, 2015) and stuffing them down only creates a blockage and/or temporary fix at best.

Emotions are just a physiological response to a situation. It is a biological chemical reaction where a multitude of hormones are flushing through our bodies at lighting speed – often in six seconds or less. A definition of e-motion is "energy in motion" and it is our body's way of communicating data with us. For example, if the new hire is getting paid more than us and we've been at the job for three years, we may get angry. Anger can be a powerful and useful emotion as the data can indicate that a boundary was crossed. When we acknowledge this anger, we might decide to do something with it and go and ask for a raise. Thus, all emotions offer us important data if we are willing to listen.

Additional Supporting Research:
- Emotional intelligence is our ability to learn from the emotional data of our own bodies along with recognizing the emotional data in others and then utilizing this to make informed decisions (Salovey & Mayer, 1990).
- Research shows that those whose emotional abilities are impaired, do not make good decisions (Apkarian, et. al., 2004). In addition, those whose have had damage in the areas of the brain where emotions are generated were unable to make any decisions (Damasio, 2000). Thus, emotions are necessary to our decision making process.

- Emotions can spread through our social networks and can be contagious (like catching a cold) and so we can be influenced by the emotional states of those around us including the emotional states of our friends, their friends' friends, and their friends' friends' friends (Fowler & Christakis, 2008).

Self-compassion and Self-kindness

Paul Gilbert, Professor of Clinical Psychology at the University of Derby described our inner voice this way: "If you have a kind, encouraging, supporting part to you, you'll be ok. If you have a bully that kicks you every time you fall over, then you're going to struggle."

Self-compassion and self-kindness are critical skills to embrace in developing as a whole human being. Our western culture is very good at developing the self-critic who chops us off at the knees before we are even ready to try and stand. Many of my coaching clients self identify with the critic voice that harbors doubt, fear, and lack of self-confidence. The critic voice says things like: "Who do you think you are?" and "What makes you think you're so special?" and "You know you're going to suck at this right?"

Researcher Kristin Neff (2011, 2013) defines self-compassion as having three core components:
- Self-kindness – This is the ability to treat ourselves kindly versus with sharp or critical self-judgment. Treating ourselves like we would treat a good friend or a person we loved – with encouragement, understanding, empathy, patience, and gentleness.
- Common Humanity – This asks us to think about "how am I the same as others?" When we look at what it means to be human, we see that at our best we are all perfectly imperfect. This is the shared human experience.

- Mindfulness – This is defined as "being with what is in the present moment." We need to turn toward and acknowledge that we are suffering in order to give ourselves compassion.

Self-compassion allows us to be authentic, unique, and our own individual self. As Oscar Wilde said, "Be yourself; everyone else is already taken." We are all different and we all experience difficulties, fear, heartache, and loss. By engaging in self-compassion and self-kindness we remain open hearted to ourselves that then allows us to be openhearted toward others.

Additional Supporting Research:
- When we criticize ourselves, we activate stress hormones that perceive threat and induce the fight/flight response. Since we are triggering this by ourselves, we become both the attacker and the victim spinning ourselves into a negative downward spiral toward depression (Neff, 2013).
- When we are kind to ourselves, we activate healing/feel good hormones that help us to feel safe so that we are in the optimum mindset to do our best (Neff, 2013).
- Research shows that self-compassionate people are motivated to learn and grow, but for intrinsic reasons, not because they want to earn social approval (Neff, 2011).

Intentional Focus and Letting in the Good

When we focus on the positive things that bring us joy, this intentional act helps us turn our regular experiences into lasting inner strengths. Dr. Rick Hanson (2013), Neuropsychologist and author, shows us that what we pay attention to is exactly how our brains are wired. Therefore, if we focus on the negative, we will see more of the negative and if we focus on the positive, we will see more of the positive. Your Joy Journal provides you with a daily practice to stop and notice the good so that you can "let it in." Your act of focusing, writing and reflection two times daily will contribute over time to rewiring your brain to actually experience more of what brings you joy, thus creating a better sense of well being.

Supporting Research:
- Neuroplasticity is the ability of the brain to change and rewire itself in response to new and different experiences (Makin, 2014).
- "Neurons that fire together, wire together" (Hanson 2013). What we pay attention to is exactly how our brains become wired.
- We need to overcome the brain's negativity bias – we are really good at learning from bad experiences, and very bad about learning from good experiences. Thus, in order to let the good "in," we need to be intentional and savor the good experience for 30-60 seconds (Hanson, 2013).
- The Law of Little Things – lots of little good experiences can add up to increased happiness (Hanson, 2013)

Social Support and Connecting with Others

"Connection is why we are here. It gives purpose and meaning to our lives" (Brown, 2010). According to Dr. Brené Brown from the University of Houston, we are social animals and survive and thrive best when we are connected to each other. Social support can be influential in how we experience different situations. When we have a strong network of one or more people that we know will have our backs, we tend to experience life as less stressful and tasks as less demanding. Throughout the Joy Journal are questions for you to reflect on how you interact with others throughout the day. The goal is to bring awareness to the idea that we can influence and cultivate more positive interactions by our thoughts, words, and deeds. Saying simple things like "please" and "thank you," or "I love you" can go along way in building deeper and more meaningful relationships.

To take this a step further, Dr. Brown said, "true belonging is a spiritual practice, and it is about the ability to find sacredness in both being a part of something but also the courage to stand alone" (2017). The Joy Journal challenges us to be our true selves and bring forth our own creativity and uniqueness. We need others to survive AND we benefit from developing our own strength and self-alliance.

Supporting Research:
- The presence and quality of supportive relationships changes our perception of challenging physical environments. People who enjoy these resources will live in a subjectively less demanding and less stressful world (Schnall et al., 2008).
- We are a social species that is totally dependent upon each other for survival. We are hardwired neurobiologically for connection and it goes against our human nature to treat each other hurtfully or violently (Forleo, 2017).

Creating New Habits: 66 days!

Many of us grew up believing that if we wanted to change a behavior or create a new one that it would take 21days for that to happen. While well intended, the magical 21 days was based on antidotal evidence gathered by Dr. Maxwell Maltz in the 1950-60's. As a plastic surgeon, Dr. Maltz noticed that his patients would take, on average; 21 days to get used their new situation (i.e. facial change, amputation). In 1960, he published his beliefs in a best selling book on behavior change called Psycho-Cybernetics. This information spread like wildfire and became indexed as common knowledge.

Jump forward 49 years and new research has been conducted to debunk the 21-day habit making myth. A team of Health Psychology researchers out of University College London led an experiment to test how long it would take participants to form an automatic response after starting something new. What they uncovered is that, on average it takes 66 days to form a new habit (Lally, et. al., 2010). They go on to report that the more complex or difficult the new habit is, the longer it will take to become routine – potentially up to 254 days!

That is why the Joy Journal was designed with 70 days of journaling pages along with multiple reflection pages. Forming a new habit takes time and intention. By participating in this Joy Journal, we are opening up to new possibilities. Oh, and the researchers also said that missing a day here and there did not mean that we have to start over on the habit forming day count. Just start again where we left off and enjoy the journey!

Finale

The world of Positive Psychology is diverse, ever growing and includes powerful research that supports us in our quest to be healthier, happier, and full-of-life human beings. There is power and healing to be found in writing down and expressing our emotions (Pennebaker, 2016) and The Joy Journal provides an outlet where we can explore and capture these joy-filled moments.

What I provided above is a tiny drop in a vast and vibrant ocean of knowledge. I hope it has wet your appetite to go out and learn more about these meaningful endeavors for yourself.

References

Apkarian, A. V., Sosa, Y., Krauss, B. R., Thomas, P. S., Fredrickson, B. E., Levy, R. E., Harden, R. N. & Chialov, D. R. (2004). Chronic pain patients are impaired on an emotional decision-making task. *Pain, 108*, 129-136.

Bekoff, M. (2007). *The emotional lives of animals: A leading scientist explores animal sorrow, and empathy – and why they matter.* Novato, CA: New World Library

Buckingham, Marcus. (2007). Strengths-based thinking and application [Video file]. Retrieved from https://www.youtube.com/watch?v=4INC6--JuoY&list=PLKWQNJHrhYCXxoUFM3GwC7Czpf vhDJtty

Burton, C. M., & King, L. A. (2009). The health benefits of writing about positive experiences: The role of broadened cognition. *Psychology & Health, 24*(8), 867-879.

Brown, B. [TED]. (June, 2010). The power of vulnerability [Video file]. Retrieved from https://www.youtube.com/watch?v=iCvmsMzlF7o

Brown, B. (2015). *Rising strong: The reckoning, the rumble, the revolution.* New York, NY: Penguin Random House.

Damasio, A. (2000). *The feeling of what happens: Body and emotion in the making of consciousness.* Orlando, FL: Harcourt, Innc.

Emmons, R. (2010). Why gratitude is good. Retrieved from https://greatergood.berkeley.edu/article/item/why_gratitude_is_good

Fearnley, R. (2014). Joy vs happiness. Retrieved from https://www.psychologies.co.uk/joy-vs-happiness

Flood, A.(2014). Unseen CS Lewis letter defines his notion of joy. Retrieved from https://www.theguardian.com/books/2014/dec/09/unseen-cs-lewis-letter-defines-joy-surprised-by-joy

Foeleo, M. (2017). Brené Brown shows you how to "Brave the Wilderness." Retrieved from https://www.youtube.com/watch?v=A9FopgKyAfl

Fowler, J. H. & Christakis, N. A. (2008). Dynamic spread of happiness in a large social network: Longitudinal analysis over 20 years in the Framingham Heart Study. *British Medical Journal, 337*. DOI: 10.1136/bmj.a2338

Fredrickson, B. L. (1998). What good are positive emotions? *Review of General Psychology, 2*(3), 300-319.

Fredrickson, B. L. (2001). The role of positive emotions in positive psychology: The broaden-and-build theory of positive emotions. *American Psychologist, 30*(3), 218-226.

Fredrickson, B. L. (2009). *Positivity.* New York, NY: Crown.

Fredrickson, B. L. [TED]. (2011). Barbara Fredrickson: Positive emotions transform us. [Video file]. Retrieved from https://www.youtube.com/watch?v=hKggZhYwoys

Fredrickson, B. L. & Losada, M.F. (2005). Positive affect and the complex dynamics of human flourishing. *American Psychologist, 60*, 678-686.

Haidt, J. (2000). The positive emotion of elevation. *Prevention and Treatment, 3*.

Hanson, R. (2013). Hardwiring happiness: Dr. Rick Hanson at TEDxMarin 2013 [Video file]. Retrieved from https://www.youtube.com/watch?v=jpuDyGgleh0

Harter, J. K., Schmidt, F. L., & Keyes, C. L. M. (2003). Well-being in the workplace and its relationship to business outcomes: A review of the Gallup studies. In Keyes, C. L. M. & & Haidt, J. (Eds.); *Flourishing: Positive psychology and the life well-lived.* Washington, DC: American Psychological Association, 205-224.

Lally, P., van Jaarsveld, C. H. M., Potts, H. W. W., & Wardle, J. (2010). How are habits formed: Modelling habit formation in the real world. *European Journal of Social Psychology, 40*(6), 998-1009. DOI: 10.1002/ejsp.674

Lambert, N. M., Gwinn, A. M., Baumeister, R. F., Strachman, A., Washburn, I. J., Gable, S. L., & Fincham, F. D. (2012) A boost of positive affect: The perks of sharing positive experiences. *Journal of Social and Personal Relationships, 30*(1), 24-43. DOI: 10.1177/0265407512449400

Losada, M. & Heaphy, E. (2004). The role of positivity and connectivity in the performance of business teams: A nonlinear dynamics model. American Behavioral Scientist. Special issue: *Contributions to Positive Organizational Scholarship, 47*(6), 740-765. DOI: 10.1177/0002764203260208

Makin, S. (2014). Blind mice cured by running: Exercise combined with visual stimulation helps to quickly restore vision in unused eyes. Scientific America. Retrieved from https://www.scientificamerican.com/article/blind-mice-cured-by-running/

Neff, K. (2011). *Self-compassion: The proven power of being kind to yourself.* New York, NY: HarperCollins.

Neff, K. [TED]. (2013). The space between self-esteem and self-compassion: Kristin Neff at TEDxCentennialParkWomen. Retrieved from https://www.youtube.com/watch?v=IvtZBUSplr4

Pennebaker, J. W. (2016). *Opening up by writing it down: How expressive writing improves health and eases emotional pain.* New York, NY: the Guilford Press.

Positive Psychology Center. (2017). Welcome. Retrieved from https://ppc.sas.upenn.edu

Salovey, P., & Mayer, J. (1990). Emotional intelligence. *Imagination, Cognition, and Personality, 9,* 185-211.

Schnall, S., Harber, K. D., Stefanucci, J. K. & Profitt, D. R. (2008). Social support and the perception of geographical slant. *Journal of Experimental Social Psychology, 44,* 1246-1255.

Tsang, J. A., Carpenter, T. P., Roberts, J. A., Frisch, M. B., & Carlisle, R. D. (2014). Why are materialists less happy? The role of gratitude and need satisfaction in the relationship between materialism and life satisfaction. *Personality and Individual Differences, 64,* 62-66. doi: 10.1016/j.paid.2014.02.009

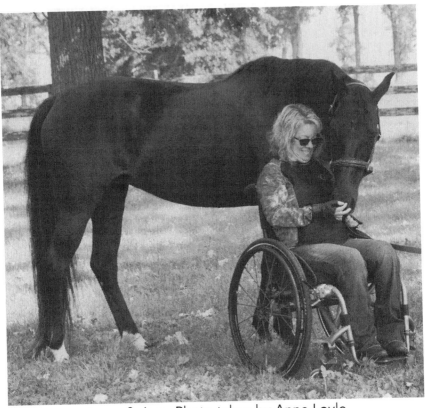

Jenny & Joy - Photo taken by Anne Loyle

To learn more, go to:
Tailfeathercoaching.com
OR
MoxieQuest.us

Join our "Cultivating Joy" community
on Facebook and share your
moments of Joy with others!

Jennifer Peterson loves finding Joy!

She is an artist, author, executive coach and speaker who empowers others to live life on purpose. She creates safe, supportive, and challenging relationships where clients can explore and find their own way to success. She is passionate about working with clients to unpack all of the "stuff" that no longer serves them in life, and then creating new habits so that they will find purpose and passion to fulfill their calling and find meaning. Jennifer uses multiple approaches (including positive psychology, biofeedback and neuroscience) to assist individuals in their own development. Her primary focus combines emotional intelligence, heart work, resilience and mindfulness to help people become aware of what is preventing them from leading the life they desire.

Jennifer's work experience includes more than 20 years of nonprofit, education, and healthcare leadership, culminating as the Executive Director for Helping Paws, a nonprofit that provides service dogs to individuals with physical disabilities. Her latest adventure includes owning a horse, Joy, and learning how to drive a carriage. She also enjoys painting, kayaking, reading, and spending time in nature and with her husband Pete and their two dogs, three cats and one horse.

Education/Certifications
- PhD in Organizational Psychology – Walden University
- Professional Certified Coach – The Hudson Institute of Santa Barbara (PCC)
- Certified Daring Way™ and Rising Strong™ Facilitator - Dr. Brené Brown
- Leadership Circle Profile™ Certification
- Shift Positive 360™ Certification
- HeartMath One-to-one Provider
- Masters in Leadership – Augsburg College

Made in the USA
Middletown, DE
24 June 2018